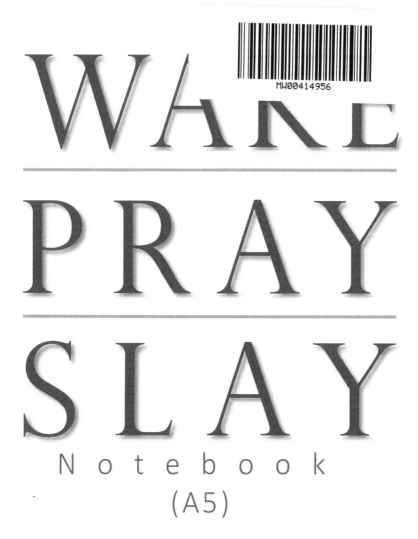

WAKE
PRAY
SLAY

Notebook
(A5)

This Book Belongs To:

www.InspirationalWares.com

InspirationalWares.com

Cute & inspirational wall art, calendars, journals and more!

For more amazing journals and adult coloring books from Penelope Pewter, visit:
Amazon.com
CreateSpace.com
InspirationalWares.com

She Believed She Could
So She Did Adult Coloring Book
with Inspirational Quotes

The Be A Pineapple
Adult Coloring Book

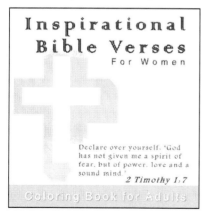

Inspirational Bible Verses
Coloring Book for Adults

The Adult Coloring Book for
Coffee Lovers

Made in the USA
Middletown, DE
26 October 2018